P9-DTQ-516

KONA
LEGENDS

KONA LEGENDS

by

Eliza D. Maguire

Illustrated by

L. R. McBride

THE PETROGLYPH PRESS
HILO
201 KINOOLE STREET 96720
HAWAII

Copyright 1966
by The Petroglyph Press, Ltd.

ISBN 912180-05-6

Sixteenth Printing
April 1991

All rights reserved.
This book, or any parts thereof may not be
reproduced without written permission.

CONTENTS

PREFACE

These few legends and stories were told us when Huehue Ranch was started in 1886. There were a number of old people living then who showed us these different places with its tales and legends.

I have translated them as they are told in the simple language of the people living amongst the rural simplicity of life, cultivating their little gardens of taro and sweet potatoes, sugar cane and bananas.

When they went to the sea-shore, they exchanged their products with those of the fishermen, and at the same time exchanged stories real and imaginary, and told legends which had been handed down by word of mouth from their ancestors, generation after generation.

The first we heard was about "Akahipuu," the hill back of the house. Then we were told of "The Cave of Makalei," where we obtained water from percolations through the roof of the cave. A redwood tank was built in the cave, and water piped to the house. The remains of a piece of ohia wood was found in the cave at that time. It may have been a part of one of the logs which Makalei's father hollowed out into a canoe, and put in the cave, as told in the story of "The Cave of Makalei."

We often repeated some of these legends and stories to visitors at the Ranch, but it was not until 1923, when Isaac W. H. Kihe, who was once a Hawaiian school teacher in this section, during the time of monarchy, began writing these tales and legends for "Ka Hoku O. Hawaii" (The Star of Hawaii), a Hawaiian weekly Hilo newspaper, edited by Reverend Stephen Desha, that I began to realize that I ought to gather and translate these stories for the future knowledge of our young children who some day may want to know about the history and legends of their own section of country.

So I have translated the legends as well as I knew, taking the best part written by Isaac Kihe, and transposing them within the meaning of what will make fairly good reading; as I lay no claim whatever to any literary ability as a translator. I just tell these legends from the simple language of my maternal tongue into the language of my paternal tongue, if it may thus be designated.

They are simple legends, relating no great deeds of warriors or the Inoa (genealogy) of high Chiefs. Those belong to historians and men of letters. Mine are tales of "Plain Every Day Folks," as we say of ordinary people, and I hope these legends will be found worth reading by "Every Day Folks."

Kekaha (barren, desolate) was the name given to that section of North Kona from Honokohau, North of Kailua, to Napuu (The Hills) meaning Puuwaawaa and Puuanahulu, and along the coast to Anaehoomalu, the boundary of South Kohala.

It is often spoken of as Kekaha-Wai-Ole (the desolate land without water). Pele, the Volcano, has literally eaten the heart out of this section.

AKAHIPUU

This is a large hill back of Huehue, and the top of it is sharp and almost pointed. It is the lowest spur of the Mountain Hualalai, and that was probably the reason it was called Akahipuu (The First Hill).

The legend tells how the little Menehune (a) wanted to take the peak of Akahipuu off and place it on the top of Kuili which is a hill below, near the sea-coast.

The hill of Kuili has a depression on its top, and the Menehune thought it would be a fine thing to take the pointed top off Akahipuu and place it in the hollow top of Kuili, for a cap.

These little Menehune were not only wonderful workers but were often mischievous, and delighted in doing all sorts of tricks.

They started to dig around the top of Akahipuu and were working away vigorously when suddenly a rooster crowed.

Down went their kauila (b) sticks which they were using as crow-bars to pry up the hill top.

The Menehune stopped working, as it was against their law to work after dawn, but they were most anxious to accomplish this undertaking, for they deemed it a fitting memorial of their great powers as supernatural beings.

They made another attempt again the second night, and again, the rooster crowed.

They were so filled with wrath over the crowing of this rooster, that they decided with one accord to catch and kill

---

(a) Menehune—Hawaiian brownies or fairies who were accredited with supernatural powers of accomplishing great things, usually in one night.
(b) Kauila—A very hard, durable wood used for spears by the ancient Hawaiian warriors.

him. They sent out three of their number. Pahulu, who was their Alii (Chief); Kuhulukoe, their Marshall, and Nahulu, the Messenger.

Now this rooster that crowed so early in the morning and prevented the Menehune from finishing their work, was also a God. His name was Moanuiahea (c) and he lived in the tall lehua forest about two miles above Akahipuu.

In the midst of this forest is a beautiful hill with a deep crater filled with ferns and luxuriant vegetation. This hill was also called Moanuiahea. Below the hill was a cave with a pool of water in it, and the rooster lived in the cave.

The water of this cave was kapu, forbidden, to women, and this rooster was the guard over this pool of water.

Kane, who was the greatest God of the forests and the waters, was the possessor of this water and it was he who placed Moanuiahea as its guard.

He also gave him orders to watch the Menehune digging around Akahipuu and to prevent them from taking its peak off and placing it on Kuili, and thus their plan for distinguishing themselves as most supernatural beings, would fall through.

Let us return and see what Pahulu, the Chief of the Menehune, and his two followers are doing.

They started, as had been arranged, to go and catch this rooster and kill him, so that their work would be accomplished. When Pahulu and his men arrived on the top of Moanuiahea Hill, they waited until the rooster should crow again; and that is also the time when the Elepaio (a Hawaiian bird) sings its olehala, last note, heralding the dawn; and the Kahuli (land shell's) piercing song is heard through the woodland.

(c) Moanuiahea—A large chicken that calls; therefore a rooster.

At last, when these signs of approaching day had died away, the rooster crowed, and these Akua (Gods) sprang up and caught and killed him.

The third night the Menehune again started digging around Akahipuu, while just below them was the imu (d) in which they had placed the rooster to kalua (bake).

The top of Akahipuu was about to be raised; the kauila sticks were in position, and just as the command was to be given, to hapai like (lift all together), the crow of a rooster was heard from the top of Moanuiahea.

They all stood aghast! Then they began to berate the three Menehune who had caught and killed the first rooster, and they said: "Why did you not see there was another rooster, and caught and killed him too?"

They argued with one another until at last they uncovered the imu and behold! No chicken in the imu!

The Menehune were so enraged at being so fooled, and deprived of their power to fulfill their desire, that they left everything as it was and fled never to appear there again. It was indeed true; the rooster Moanuiahea had come to life again. The God Kane had seen him killed, so he gave him the water of life, and thus he lived again.

After the Menehune had left Akahipuu, Kaleikini, a person of power and renown, a distinguished warrior, came and with a kauila rod, thrust it nine feet deep, and fastened the hill down firm so that the Menehune could not come again and take it away.

This kauila log was in the side of the hill when we first came to live at Huehue, but now there is no trace of any kauila. A forest of eucalyptus, pine, kukui and other trees cover the whole hill.

(d) Imu—An oven in the ground filled with hot stones, upon which food is cooked.

THE FISH POND OF PAAIEA

This was a very large fish-pond extending from Kaele-huluhulu, adjoining the little fishing hamlet of Mahaiula, and as far as Wawaloli on the boundary of Ooma.

This pond was not far from Ka-Lae-O-Keahole, (Fisherman's Point) which is the extreme Western point, or cape on the Island of Hawaii, and on which there is a lighthouse.

To mariners of the days of sailing crafts, this point was a test of skillful navigation; the wind and tide and current, all combining to thwart the mariner's effort to round the cape, and make the entrance into Kailua Bay.

This Fish-Pond of Paaiea was three miles long, and a mile and a half wide. The fishermen going to Kailua and further South, often took a short cut by taking their canoes into the pond and going across, thus saving time and the hard labor of paddling against the Eka (a) and also against the strong current from Keahole.

This fish-pond belonged to a certain Chief, and it was well guarded.

No one was allowed to take or eat a fish without the Chief's permission, and from him to the Konohiki (Overseer).

There were houses for the guards and the Overseer of the fish-pond.

This Konohiki or Overseer's name was Kepaalani, and under him were the stewards and other servants of the Chief.

(a) Eka—A strong sea breeze from the South.

One day an old woman appeared at the large canoe shed of Kepaalani.

The canoes had come in with a large catch of fish, Aku, (Bonito) and the fishermen were cleaning and salting them, and preparing them for drying.

This was the season for Aku, along the Kona coast, and the canoes were filled with fish.

When the people saw this strange woman decorated with a wreath of Kookoolau (b), they greeted her "Aloha!" and she returned their greeting, "Aloha!"

A man by the name of Kapulau said to her: "Malihini?" (stranger).

She replied "I am a kamaaina, (c), not exactly a total stranger, but I do not often come down here to the seashore.

"Living in the restful uplands, and hearing that there was plenty of fish down at the beach, I hastened down to see if the fishermen would give me a bit of palu (d)."

Kapulau answered: "There is plenty of fish and plenty of palu, but we have not the right to give the fish or palu; the Konohiki is the one who has that right. He is sitting over there, and you go and ask him."

The old woman went away, and to the great astonishment of every one, they saw a great crowd of people following her.

When she appeared before Kepaalani, he asked: "A stranger? From where?"

She replied: "From the tangled wilds of the uplands. Hearing of the great quantity of fish down here at the beach I came to get a few."

(b) Kookoolau—A wild shrub with pretty yellow flowers, used dried as a tea.
(c) Kamaaina—A resident; well known in the place.
(d) Palu—The intestines of the fish.

"No fish," replied the stern Overseer.

"The fish is given to the men of the Chief. I am only a guardian."

"Well! If there is no fish, give me a bit of palu."

"There is no palu; all given to the men of the Chief."

"Then give me a few opae (shrimps) from the pond of the Chief."

"No! You cannot have fish, palu, shrimps or anything. It all belongs to the Chief, and only the Chief can give them to you.

"Well! That is all. I now return to the uplands without even a grain of salt." The old woman stood up and turned around to go.

When she had gone quite a distance, another great crowd was seen walking around the edge of the pond.

When she came to Kapulau's house, she was urged to remain and have something to eat. She consented and sat down. When she had finished her meal, Kapulau gave her a fish.

The old woman stood up, and before starting to go, she gave these instructions to her host:

"Tonight, you and your wife put up a lepa (e) back of your house, and here on your fence; for it is said, there will be a night of great doings, and tonight may be the night, and you will have your unuunu (protection) ready against any evil befalling you."

She turned around and started to go up, but mysteriously disappeared.

Not a sign of anyone to be seen by the people who were watching for her appearance on the plains above.

That night, the people living at the beach, saw a fire

(e) Lepa—A piece of kapa (Hawaiian cloth) tied at the end of a stick as a kapu (forbidden) sign.

on the Mountain of Hualalai, and as they saw it coming down its slopes, they realized that the old woman whose request for fish, palu and shrimps had been refused, could have been no other than the Goddess Pele (f).

The lava came and destroyed the great fish-pond of Pa-aiea, dried its water and filled and covered it with black rocks.

That is the way the Goddess Pele avenged herself on those who did not acknowledge her as Supreme, and refused to grant her slightest wish.

(f) Pele—The volcano fabled as a Goddess.

THE TWO GIRLS ROASTING BREAD-FRUIT

The legend of The Fish Pond of Paaiea, in the preceding chapter, tells how an old woman appeared before the fishermen asking for fish, and was told that they would give her nothing, and how, when she left them to go to her home in the mountains, she mysteriously disappeared.

This same old woman soon afterwards appears at a village called Manuahi which was on the Western slope of Hualalai, and where these two girls who figure in this story, lived.

When this remarkable old woman arrived at the village, it was quite deserted and only two girls were there and they were roasting bread-fruit.

The name of one of these girls was Pahinahina and the name of the other was Kolomu'o.

As soon as the old woman saw them she inquired: "For whom are you roasting your bread-fruit?"

The girl named Kolomu'o answered: "I am roasting my bread-fruit for La'i."

"Who is La'i?"

"That is my God."

"Yes? Has La'i power?"

"Yes, that is the God of my parents."

Then the old woman turned and asked Pahinahina, the other girl, "and for whom, pray, are you roasting your bread-fruit?"

"For Pele," she said.

"Well, if that is so, it is our bread-fruit, and it is cooked."

"I do not think it can be cooked, it has only just been turned over."

"Yes, it is cooked, it is smoking."

When they tasted it, sure enough, it was cooked and they ate all of it.

Then the old woman asked her: "Where is your house?"

"Above there, near that hill."

"And where is the house of this other girl?"

"We all live in one house with our parents, she at one end of the house with her parents."

"Where are your parents?"

"Gone to clear land around to plant for the Chief."

"When your parents come home, you tell them to put up a lepa (sign) on the end of your part of the house."

When her parents came home, Pahinahina told them the instructions this old woman had given her, and they followed it out.

Mysterious instructions of that nature were always followed out, as people of those days believed that only supernatural beings or Gods gave instructions in that manner.

That night, after this old woman's visit to the Fish-Pond of Paaiea, and her interview with the two girls roasting bread-fruit, she appeared as none other than Pele, the Goddess of the Volcano, who lived at Kilauea.

She evidently was in the habit of traveling about and taking up her abode wherever she fancied, and in 1801 she came over to Hualalai Mountain and started her devilish work.

The people, that night, saw a fire on Hualalai, at a place called Ka-Waha-O-Pele, (The Mouth of Pele) and thought it was the fire of the bird catchers of the Ua'u.(a) Then the fire disappeared, and again lower down, burst forth where the scrub lehua and ferns grew, a place called Ka-Iwi-O-Pele, (The Back-bone of Pele) and it was thought to be a camp fire of the canoe builders.

There the fire flared brightly, then it dwindled down and went out. Soon after, it appeared below Kileo, one of the many spurs of Hualalai, and about a quarter of a mile to the right of Akahipuu, coming out of a little opening and flowing in a thin stream of lava, spreading and growing larger until it covered the South end of the girls' house.

Pele continued her course to the sea and finished her work of destruction.

The cinder hill of Puhi-A-Pele, (Pele's Bon-Fire) which looms like a huge castle of ebony, showing in strong relief against the silvery kukui (b) grove above it, represents the home of one of the two girls roasting bread-fruit which Pele destroyed.

It is, at present, a striking landmark plainly visible, about a mile below the road, as one crosses the ridge of the Kona Mountain.

(a) Ua'u—A species of bird that dives in the sea for fish and takes it to the mountain to eat.

(b) Kukui—Candle nut tree.

THE POOL OF WAWALOLI

This little pool of water is situated near the sea-shore between Ooma and Kaloko. The story of this pool has been handed down from generations past to the present day, and is related thus:

Wawaloli was the name of a certain Loli (a sea slug). He was a kupua (a wizard). He had two bodies, a limpsy fish body and the body of a man.

There lived in the uplands covered with ilima (a), a man by the name of Kaluaolapa and his wife, and their beautiful and charming daughter, Malumaluiki.

One day she said to her mother that she was going to the beach to gather limu, (sea-wead), opihi, and pupu (b). Her mother said she could go.

So she went down, and feeling thirsty, she stopped at the pool to take a drink. She knelt down and, stooping over, drank the cool water.

While she was drinking, she noticed the water began to bubble, and at the same time a shadow was cast over her, and turning around, she saw a handsome young man smiling graciously at her.

"Pardon me," he said, "for intruding upon you in this spot where your beautiful form and face was reflected in the clear depths of this pool."

"Why apologize?" the beautiful girl answered. "We

(a) Ilima—A shrub whose flowers strung, make the yellow lei (wreath) which is now copied with paper.
(b) Opihi and pupu—Species of shell fish much relished by Hawaiians.

11

both are strangers to each other, and we meet as strangers at this pool."

The young man again replied, looking at her with adoring eyes, for she was truly very beautiful: "I am no stranger along these shores. I am a kamaaina, and this is my home, and because I saw you coming down here I came to meet you."

Having thus met they abandoned themselves to the witcheries of love; and the beautiful girl, forgetting her longing for the sea-weed and shell fish, for which she came to the sea-shore, cast her net for more captivating fish. Oblivious of everything, wrapt in their own enchantment, time sped on, and the rays of the sinking sun in the Western horizon, at last awoke them to the realities of life, and that it was time to part.

Before the girl started on her homeward way, the young man asked her name, and she told him her name was Malumaluiki.

"My name," he said, "when we are together is Wawa, but my name when you come and sit by the pool you must call Loli, and you must call out these words:"

> "E Loli Nui kikewekewe
> I ka hana ana kikewekewe
> I kuu piko kikewekewe
> A ka makua kikewekewe
> I hana ai kikewekewe
> E pii mai oe kikewekewe
> Ka kaua puni kikewekewe
> Puni Kauoha kikewekewe."

TRANSLATION

"O Great Loli, Charmer, Charmer!
Cast thy spell, O Charmer, Charmer,
Of enchantment, Charmer, Charmer,
Over me, O Charmer, Charmer!
Come hither, Charmer, Charmer,
To our tryst, O Charmer, Charmer;
Your heart's desire, Charmer, Charmer,
Awaits you, O Charmer, Charmer."

"O Loli Dear! Behold your heart's desire, your charming one, Malumaluiki, over whom your spell has cast its witching glamour!"

When this compact had been made, the beautiful girl departed, and just at dusk, as the lights were lit in the house, she arrived home.

Her parents inquired: "Why! where are your opihi, limu and a bit of pupu?"

She answered: "That you should ask me when the beach was full of people, and they had gathered everything before I got down there. I could not find a single opihi, not a shred of limu, and not even a scrap of anything, so I came home."

As supper was ready, she sat down and ate, and very shortly she arose.

"Finished your supper already?" said her mother.

"I am not hungry; my legs are so tired walking so much today, she said," and went straight to bed, but there was no sleep for her; she tossed and mused and was so consumed with the flames of love, that she could not sleep that night.

At break of day she was up and started again for the beach.

When she arrived at the pool, she slid into the water, and started to call as she had been taught on the previous day, and immediately this Loli appeared in the form of the handsome youth of the day before.

Another day was spent in love making, and so it continued for several days.

In the meantime, the parents of the girl were puzzled over their daughter's actions in wandering to the beach every day and remaining until dusk, and coming home without anything.

So they resolved to spy on her. The next day the father followed his daughter down and saw her reclining on the edge of the pool and heard her call.

"O Great Loli, Charmer, Charmer!
Cast thy spell, O Charmer, Charmer,
Of enchantment, Charmer, Charmer,
Over me, O Charmer, Charmer!
Come hither, Charmer, Charmer,
To our tryst, O Charmer, Charmer;
Your heart's desire, Charmer, Charmer,
Awaits you, O Charmer, Charmer."

"O Loli Dear! Behold your heart's desire, your charming one, Malumaluiki, over whom your spell has cast its witching glamour!"

The father then saw a Loli come out of a hole in the pool and change into a human being. He saw his daughter wrapt in the embrace of this being having two bodies, and bestowing caresses upon her with all a lover's ardent fervor, oblivious of everything but their own desires.

The father returned home and told the mother all that he had seen and heard, and when she heard it, she was very

15

sad and at the same time very wroth with her daughter's disgraceful conduct.

When her husband told her what sort of a lover their daughter had, a double bodied being, a loli! she told him to go back and catch this loli and beat him to death; and her husband agreed to do so.

The next day he followed his daughter and hid without her seeing him, and he listened intently to the words of his daughter's call, and learned them by heart. After his daughter had started up for home, he went and looked into the pool, and saw a round circle on the water, and he knew there must be a hole below from which that loli came up.

He slept that night, and the next day, at dawn he went to the pool with his trapping net and went into the pool giving the call his daughter said, imitating the tone of her voice as nearly as possible.

As soon as he had finished, the loli came out of his hole, and was caught in the ensnaring net and Kaluaolapa quickly wound the net around so that the loli could not escape.

As he was going up, he saw his daughter coming down, so he hid until she had passed.

When the girl reached the pool she started her usual call. Nothing appeared. She again called and repeated her call until the sun was high in the heavens; not a sign of loli, the limpsy fish body, or Wawa, the human body.

Thinking him dead she started her wailing, moans, and sobs, calling for her lover in endearing names and bewailing her great loss.

Late in the evening, giving up hope, she returned to her home.

Let us return to where we left Kaluaolapa with the loli in the net. When he arrived home and showed it to his wife she said to him: " Take it to the kahuna (witch doctor) Papaapoo who is staying at Hoohila."

When Papaapoo saw the loli in the net and heard the whole story, he told them to prepare an imu and bake this "Great Loli, Charmer, Charmer."

When this loli is dead, your daughter will live on, and so will all the daughters of the families around here.

They heated the imu and cooked the enchanted loli.

When the daughter returned home, her eyes were swollen with weeping. Her mother asked her "Why are your eyes so swollen, my daughter?"

She did not answer but hung her head.

The father came in and seeing his daughter with her head down, said: "Yes! Your lover with whom you were daily meeting and making clandestine love, is held by the kahuna, Papaapoo, and is now being cooked in the imu, so that you and all the other girls with whom this loli has been making love, may live!"

This pool is still to be seen with the round hole out of which the "Great Loli, Charmer, Charmer," came.

THE CAVE OF MAKALEI

This cave is situated a little above the right of Akahipuu, the hill back of the home of Huehue Ranch.

There once lived near this cave a man by the name of Ko'amokumoku-o-heeia.

He came as a stranger from Koolau, Oahu, and settled here with his wife, whose name was Kahaluu, two daughters and his youngest child, a son named Makalei.

When this man settled in this place, he began to cultivate taro (a), sweet potatoes, bananas, sugar cane and awa (b), which all grew without water. The people who had always lived in this part of the country came and told him that the great drawback to this section was no water, except in celebrated caves which are kapu (forbidden).

They told him that if he were to get water by stealth from a celebrated cave, and he was found out, he would be killed by the owner of that cave.

When he heard this, he made troughs to catch the water, and when the rains came, he filled his calabashes and troughs.

One day this little boy, Makalei, went to throw some refuse in a sort of hollow, back of the house, and while he was digging around, a cold wind suddenly rushed up, and looking down, he saw a very deep hole.

He was only a little fellow, about three or four years old, and although the wind rushed out and almost took his

---

(a) Kalo or taro—A species of arum esculentum, the well known vegetable from which poi, the staple food of the Hawaiians, is made.

(b) Awa—A plant, the roots of which is made into a stupefying drink.

19

breath away, he was not frightened, but went to his father who was in his garden and said: "I went over there, and while I was digging around a great wind came out of a hole. There must be a wind cave over there."

"Where is it?" asked his father.

"Down there," said the little boy.

His father went to look at what his son had discovered. When Ko-amokumoku-o-heeia arrived at the place his son pointed out to him, he lifted some large slabs of stone which partly closed the hole, and he saw a deep cave extending far in, and a cold wind rushed out as if from the mountain. He turned to his son and said: "We have found our own celebrated cave of water in this dry country, and I dedicate it to you. It shall be called "He Ano O Makalei." (c)

"I will fix it so that no one will ever find it." He fixed one side of the entrance of the cave for a rubbish heap, and put a large slab of stone so that the opening of the cave on the other side could not be seen. He told his little son not to tell anyone, not even his mother.

The next day Ko'amokumoku-o-heeia went in by himself. The opening, even to this day, is low, and he crawled in on his hands and knees, and when he got in, he found it a large cave extending far in, for quite a distance. He could stand upright and not touch his head to the top of the cave.

Drops of water were dripping from the roof of the cave, and running down the sides.

He made up his mind to hollow out canoes of ohia (d) and wiliwili (e) and fill them with water. He went into

---

(c) He Ano O Makalei—Consecrated to Makalei. The word ana means cave, but ano literally is the form or appearance of a person or thing. He ano means to set apart, to consecrate.

(d) Ohia—Metrosideros. Native forest trees of hard wood from which canoes were hollowed.

(e) Wiliwili—Erythina. A soft white wood used for the outriggers of canoes.

this cave at night, carrying in logs of wiliwili and hollowed them out, but the ohia logs, he placed in the middle of his garden, hidden by his banana and awa plants. When he had hollowed out the ohia logs, in the shape of canoes, he took them into the cave during the night. The wiliwili logs being light, he hollowed into small troughs, so that he could carry them out filled with water, while the ohia canoes remained as storage containers. He filled the cave with great numbers of canoes, and the interior of the cave was strewn with wiliwili troughs and ohia canoes.

When the dry weather came, which often lasts for months in this section of Kona, he had nothing to worry about. He went in at night and filled his troughs, calabashes and other containers, and had all the water he wanted for drinking and domestic use. The kamaaina were bewildered, and wondered where this stranger got his water from, as there were no signs of water to be found around the place.

Some years afterwards, this family moved to Kauai, and someone else came and lived there, but evidently all traces of the opening of this cave were hidden by the rubbish heap and the koali (wild morning glory) vines had grown and twined all over the opening of the cave.

One day there was a great celebration given in honor of some occasion, and all sorts of games and sports were being held. A fine looking young man, a stranger to the crowd, came there and entered into the sports. He seemed to be winning a number of the games. This peeved many of the kamaaina youths, especially as the admiration of the women were bestowed on this stranger.

In the intermission between the games, the young man

asked for a drink of water. He was told this was a land of no water, especially now, as it was the dry season, and the only water to be found was at the beach where fresh water bubbled out of the sea. The young man said there was water there; the owner of the place denied the assertion, and back and forth they contradicted each other, until the landlord grew very angry, and the crowd cried out to beat and kill this fellow.

He said he would find the water for them; and so it was agreed that if he found the water, the landlord would give one of his beautiful daughters in marriage to him, but if he did not find any water, he would be beaten to death.

He at once went to the rubbish heap, and began to clear it amidst the jeers of the onlookers. A man feeling sorry for the handsome youth laboring so hard to clear all that filth out, set to and helped him. After a while to the great surprise of every one, the mouth of a cave opened out, and following the young man in, they found the floor of the cave strewn with canoes filled with water, clear and cold.

This young man then told them the story of the founding of this cave, and that it was named for him.

"He Ano O Makalei." (Consecrated to Makalei.)

Makalei married the beautiful maiden, but returned with her to Kauai.

The cave is known to this day as the Cave of Makalei.

MANINIOWALI

There is a little bay by this name of Maniniowali (a) situated between Kukio and Awakee. This bay is like a turquoise gem along this barren lava coast. The water is always a turquoise blue. There is a stone in the form of a woman imbedded in the sand at the edge of the beach, which also bears the name of Maniniowali. The legend of this stone is as follows:

There were two families living along these lands by the sea, and they were neighbors.

A son was born to one family and he was named Uluweuweu, and his home was at Kukio. A daughter was born, the same day, to the other family, and she was named Maniniowali, and her home was at Maniniowali Bay. The parents at their birth declared them betrothed.

They grew to manhood and womanhood. He was fine in form and face, and skilled in the sports of men of those times.

The girl was very beautiful according to the old Hawaiian type, round and full in form and features.

When the time of the "hoao," (announcement of betrothal) was near, great preparations were made for a large feast. The day before the announcement when everything was ready, Uluweuweu, the young man, was suddenly taken ill. The celebration was then postponed.

When the young man found that the engagement festivities had been put off, he grew well as quickly as he had

(a) Manini-O-Wali—A string of Manini. A species of fish, flat in shape and of a greenish gray color with dark stripes around its body.

23

fallen ill, and he was seen to lelekawa and heenalu (b). As soon as the folks saw he was well, they began preparations again, for the second time. Again the young man fell ill and nearly died, as they all thought.

For this extraordinary illness of Uluweuweu, a kahuna whose name was Kikaua, was sent for.

When he entered the house, Uluweuweu sat up and said to every one around: "Why are you all here? I am not sick."

"Why?" the mother replied. "Because we saw you all doubled up with pain, so we sent for Kikaua, the kahuna."

The doctor then said: "The boy is not physically ill; he is, to sum up the whole matter, lovesick."

Everyone was speechless with astonishment. Then the kahuna said: "You all hear what the matter is with the boy. He is in the thrills of first love; the lovelorn looks, sighs and yearnings for the love that reigns within his heart; now burning, now cold as the snow of Mauna Kea; the sleepless nights, roaming together with the 'Ipo Lei Manu,' (Sweet Love Bird), until the fragrance of dawn is wafted on the zephyrs of the morn.

"Thus it is—A beautiful flower has been disclosed to him; he muo (c) blossoming into the height of perfection.

"That is the spider that has ensnared into her web this bird of the sea-spray and drawn him into the meshes of the net in the mists of the uplands."

When the kahuna had finished speaking these riddles, a buzz went around the assembly; questions were asked of each other.

(b) Lelekawa—To drive off from a high place. Heenalu—to ride the breakers on a surf-board.

(c) He muo—Literally, a bud; figuratively, a growing child, especially of a Chief; in this instance, a young Princess.

"Who can this person be the kahuna is referring to? Who can guess?"

The kahuna then said: "It is none other than the brilliant daughter of Poopoomino and Kaeleawaa, High Chiefs, and her name is Kahawaliwali."

She was a beautiful Princess, and they had been holding clandestine meetings without any suspicion of their tryst, until the kahuna brought it out to the knowledge of every one.

Amongst those in the assembly who heard the exposé of the kahuna, were relatives of the parents of Maniniowali, and they went and told them all that they had heard from the kahuna.

"So the daughter's betrothed is not ill but just in love!"

"In love with whom?" asked the mother.

"In love with the Princess Kahawaliwali; and here we have been thinking he was really ill, but he was only pretending, in order to put off his betrothal ceremonies with Maniniowali."

As soon as the mother had heard of this scandal, she immediately went to the parents of the young fellow and told them that the engagement was cancelled and they would have nothing more to do with such a deceitful fellow.

The parents of the boy could not do otherwise than consented to the breaking off of the betrothal.

When Maniniowali heard all this, and that her betrothal was ended, she became very ill, and Kikaua was sent for.

When the kahuna came and saw her, he said: "Well, I thought she was really ill, but no, she is heart-broken; disappointed love!"

The kahuna turned to her parents and said: "I have two propositions to place before you. The first is to have the announcement of the betrothal immediately made, without waiting any longer. Second—do away with them all! Which do you choose?"

The mother answered: "Do away with them all!"

"That is the decree!" said the kahuna; and he immediately began to work his black art. He is told as having prayed to his Gods, the Goddess Pele being the principal one, and the young girls and the young man were all disposed of.

Uluweuweu was turned into a stone which is seen standing at the edge of the sea to this day. He stands on the shore, his lower limbs firm and fast, and where the upper part is joined to the firm rock in the ground, is a groove like a door hinge which rocks back and forth when the waves dash against it.

Kahawaliwali, the Princess, was turned into a long stone about thirty feet high, which stands in the sea. The lower part has two sections, and it is said they represent her legs through which the sea flows continually.

Maniniowali, however, was alert and ran and laid down on the sand at the edge of the sea, so when she was turned into a stone she was firm in the sand. When the tide comes in, she is covered, and when the tide goes out the sand is washed away and her form is seen lying clearly outlined on the beach.

But the strangest thing of all is; a kaawili (school) of manini, in a line so close together that it looks like a string, or a long fish resembling a shark, trails across this little bay of Maniniowali from end to end.

During the evenings of Ku, that is when the moon is in the West at sunset, this string of manini is seen; also in the mornings of Lono and Mauli (d) they follow in a long line. It is said that this Maniniowali (twist or string of manini) is the girl's fish body and she was called that name on that account, and that is why the manini strings across this bay named after her.

(d) Lono—When the moon is on the wane. Mauli—When the moon is on the wane, just before the end.

THE WATERS OF KANE

There is a spring of fresh water which bubbles out of the sand along the edge of the sea, on the beach of Kaupulehu. There is a legend connected with the gushing forth of this spring of water. It dates way back to the time when soothsayers, magicians, and the ancient Gods had their sway; long before Pele, the Goddess of Fire, had come and taken possession of the country from the top of Hualalai to the sea-coast.

The legend relates that, at that time, there was a Chiefess controlling the great division of the land of Kaupulehu, and the adjoining lands of Kukio and Maniniowali. She was ruler over thousands of people and the land around was well cultivated.

There came at one time during the reign of the Chiefess, a great drought. The sweet potato gardens, the taro patches; these principal vegetables which furnished the daily food of the Chiefess and her retainers, and her people, were all dried up.

When the last potato and taro were gone, they ate the hapuu (the root of the tree fern), the ma'u, (the root of a fern smaller than the tree fern), the pala, (the root of another variety of fern), the pia, (arrowroot), the hoi (a) and the noni (b).

The sun continued to scorch everything. At last there was nothing to eat. The people grew hollow-eyed and were so weak from hunger that they fell down and slept.

_____

(a) Hoi—The bulbous root of a vine eaten in time of scarcity, acrid to the taste.
(b) Noni—A shrub whose fruit is large and yellow, often used for medicine, not very palatable.

When the Chiefess saw the awful condition of her people, she asked her Kahuna, a Priest who had communication with the Gods, to intercede for her and her people. "Ask the Gods to show us the way to obtain life," she said to him. The kahuna looked on his magic board, and after a while he replied: "O Chiefess! The signs show there is no more life, but it is up to you to consider what sins you have committed, that this great affliction should have been put upon you and your people, and to give your consent to the expiation of your faults; and then, only then, can you, your people and your land have life."

The Chiefess bowed her head, meditating on what she had just heard from the lips of her Kahuna.

Raising her head, she asked the Priest: "What am I to consent to do for the atonement of my sins in order to gain life for me and my people, and to recover the land from endless destruction?"

The Priest replied. "These are the terms imposed upon you: Remain kapu (c) and pray for forgiveness during one anahulu (d), at the same time implore your brother, Poohuna (e) in these words:

'O Kane, the God of Living Waters!

O Kane, the Life Giver of our world!

Give unto me and all my people, a great life, a long life, and replenish our land with the life-giving fruits of abundance!' "

The Chiefess heard these words of her Kahuna, and she obeyed his instructions, remaining kapu for ten days, at the end of which time, having purified herself, she came forth cleansed from all unrighteousness.

(c) Kapu—A state of fasting and restriction from intercourse with anyone.
(d) Anahulu—A period of time, (ten days).
(e) Poohuna—Literally (hidden head). An appellation of one of the Gods —namely, Kane of the Living Waters.

The next day a man was seen coming down from the plains above, a stranger to the people.

When he came into the presence of the Chiefess, she recognized him as her Godly brother to whom she had been praying for aid, Kane of the Living Waters. She sprang up and kissed her brother.

Kane asked: "What is all this trouble over the land and the people of the Chiefess?"

"What indeed, but a terrible affliction has befallen upon us and all the country around! The sun has dried up all living plants, the earth is so parched nothing will grow, we have no food, no water, we are all faint and dizzy and cannot walk and are lying down nigh unto death."

"You are indeed in great pilikia (trouble)," said Kane.

"I knew you must be in trouble, because these signs which I feel always foretell trouble, and they urge me to go forth and locate them. The hair on my head began to eeu (creep) and ka loku o ka poli o kuu wawae (the arch of my feet ached) so I knew you were in trouble and needed me and I came to find out."

Kane called all the men who were able to walk to go and get plenty of firewood. There were about a thousand or more who went for firewood.

(He mau lau). Lau is four hundred; mau means more than two, so there must have been a thousand or more who had strength to go. We must remember that Kane was the Great Life Giving God, and probably gave these men strength to gather firewood.

When the men returned with a great pile of firewood Kane told them to make an imu. The men did as they were instructed. When the imu was intensely hot, Kane told them to bring akulikuli (f) and makaloa (g) and great quantities of these things were brought.

Kane then said: "Ulu ka imu." (h).

But what seemed strange, no food was seen put into the imu after the embers and ashes were thrown out.

Kane still directed them: "Put on the akulikuli and the makaloa; spread them thick."

When spread, Kane laid down on the imu and told them, "Put on dirt and makaloa until I am covered out of sight."

The men put on the dirt and makaloa; and the more they put on the higher grew the imu, until at last they gave up trying to cover it.

While the men were shouting over this man being buried in the imu, Kane appeared from below and demanded the imu to be uncovered, and the strange imu was immediately uncovered. When it was laid bare there was heaped up food all cooked.

One side had taro, another potatoes, bread-fruit, yam, arrowroot; and all these things were ready, and the people sat down and ate; and what was left over, the Kahuna divided it all around.

When Kane laid down on the imu he appeared in the sea, and the opening where he came forth again was a bubbling spring, and it was called The Waters of Kane.

On account of Kane being pulehu (roasted) in the imu, this beach is called Kaupulehu (i), and not only the beach but the great division of land from the mountain to the sea.

(f) Akulikuli—A kind of water herb.
(g) Makaloa—A kind of rush from which very fine mats are made.
(h) "Ulu ka imu"—Throw out the embers and ashes, ready for putting in food to cook.
(i) Kaupulehu—Literally, Ka-imu-pulehu A-Ke-Akua. The oven in which the God was roasted.

THE CATCH OF THE GODS

In olden days, at the fishing hamlet of Makalawena, the story is told of mysterious fishing with supernatural beings.

The fishermen casting their net at night would think that those alongside of them were their own fellow companions. The net would be dragged down with the weight of the fish, but as soon as the net was hauled ashore, not a single fish would be in it. The fishermen would sometimes dive down when the net felt heavy, but the sea would flash and flame like forks of lightning (a) and dazzle their eves, so that they could see nothing.

This happened so frequently that the fishermen were exasperated, and held council to decide on a plan for exterminating these devilish Akua.

They decided to get Puniaiki of Kohala, for he was renowned as a destroyer of Akua; he knew how to catch them.

A messenger was sent to Kohala. When he arrived in Kohala, he made inquiries as to where Puniaiki was to be found. He was shown the way to his house, and on meeting Puniaiki, he related to him the object of his visit.

Puniaiki said to him: "Tomorrow we start, as this day is over, and we must not travel at night; in the meantime we will weave a net to catch the gods."

The messenger replied: "Why waste time making a net? My house is filled with nets of every description."

"Maybe nets only in quantity, but not the quality that

(a) This probably was due to the phosphorescence, but the legend relates it as the work of the Akua-devils.

would catch Akua or devils; for how is it you have not been able to catch them," said Puniaiki.

They wove a net of the very finest mesh, and when finished they put it in a hokeo (b) so that the Akua could not see it.

Early the next morning they started, following the seacoast till they came to a place called Kaiopae, and found a canoe going to Kekaha, North Kona, to fish for ahi (albicore) and they got on as far as Makalawena, and went ashore.

When they landed, Puniaiki told his companion not to tell anyone a single thing about him, or about his journey to Kohala, not even to call his name, Puniaiki, but to call him Kalepeamoa, cock's-comb, on account of his bald head.

Puniaiki, or Kalepeamoa as we shall now call him, began getting acquainted with the people. He told his friend to prepare the nets, and instruct certain ones to take turns as Kapeku (c). There were to be two shifts of splashers.

The night shift would be those who were to begin with him in the early part of the night, and the day shift at the finish.

The splashers were all to sleep during the day. Then at night, one set was to start with him, but they were to splash the water only on the edge; he alone was to swim out with the fine meshed net.

When he gave one whistle then one splasher was to dive and swim out to him; when he whistled again two were to swim out, whistled again, three, and so on until all the splashers of the night shift were out; then all the splashers of the day shift were to join in pulling in the net.

(b) Hokeo—A long gourd or calabash used by the Hawaiian fishermen for carrying fishing tackle.
(c) Kapeku—Splashers. Those who splash the water to drive the fish into the net.

The splashers were all ready, and Kalepeamoa walked out, while he saw the Akua, little devils, watching him.

Then he swam out beyond his depth and whistled. Instantly one of these devils jumped into the fine meshed net, and Puniaiki rolled and strangled him to death.

He whistled again; another little devil jumped in and was finished in the same manner, and so on until five kauna (d) were caught. Then Puniaiki called to the splashers whom he had left for the last, to come out with their net and they all swam out and let the net down and dragged in this big catch of the gods.

The fishermen had no more trouble in filling their nets with fish, as they were rid of the little devils.

The place has ever since been called Kuuna-A-Ke-Akua, The Catch of the Gods.

(d) Kauna—A group of 4, so 5 kauna would be 20.

THE HILL OF MOEMOE

Moemoe was the name of a prophet who was under the command of the Goddess Pele. The legend relates how this prophet, Moemoe, saved the population of Napuu (The Hills), meaning Puuanahulu, and Puuwaawaa, from being devoured by a Shark-God who inhabited that part of the country. He was also a kukini makanipuahiohioi (a whirlwind runner). The hill of Moemoe was named after hm, and there was a say¹ng about the hill of Moemoe with reference to the person Moemoe.

"Brush of Moemoe, brush of Moemoe. Where is Moemoe?" The brush of Moemoe answers:

"Gone long ago; only the day is left to me."

Moemoe was so swift, he was gone long before the rays of the sun could touch him or the flat hill of Moemoe.

When Moemoe, the prophet, arrived at this hill, and sat down to rest, he heard the sound of voices loudly talking as they were rushing down to the beach. He turned around and saw a great crowd of people talking excitedly, so he went to see what it was all about.

When he arrived there, a great crowd was gathered around, and he beheld a game of konane (a) being played on the papa konane of the Chief Ka'ualii and the Chiefess Welewele. When he came nearer, he found one of the players was a man from the uplands of Napuu, whose name was Iwahaonou (b), and he recognized him as a two bodied

---

(a) Konane—Hawaiian checkers played on a stone checker-board (papakonane) with shells.
(b) Iwahaonou—(Literally, stuffed mouth) a mouthful.

39

being, a human body and a shark body. The people did not suspect this Iwahaonou as anything else than a man, but Moemoe recognized him right away as a aiwaiwa (c), sitting there as a human being, but capable of turning into a shark, and devouring all these people around him.

As soon as Moemoe sat down, Iwahaonou began immediately to quiz him.

"Say! Do you know the No'a (d), if not, perhaps the konane?"

Moemoe answered: "I have learned all those games; also the kukini, the kilokilo ouli (e); to prophesy the weather, storms and calm; to predict the future, life or death; to know the appearance of a man, woman, child, old man and bent and crippled old woman."

"Yes! You do know a great deal! You can fathom from childhood to old age when the eyes are dim, the steps totter, and the breath is short! Indeed! And pray, who are you and what is your name?"

"I am not going to tell you my name, until you tell me yours first, for that was not your first question; the no'a and the konane was what you wanted to match your skill with mine; and let me tell you, I can just knock this coward of a braggart clean over the Pukolu (f) like the wind of Launiu; you hear me!"

Iwahaonou tried to pass it off, but not so the assembly. With one accord they shouted in favor of Moemoe to konane.

When Iwahaonou saw that the crowd favored the malihini (stranger) he said: "I am going to ask you, nameless

(c) Aiwaiwa—A fabulous person.
(d) No'a—A game of hiding a stone called Noa and guessing where to find it.
(e) Kilokilo—Prophesying (ouli—omens); predicting omens.
(f) Pukolu—The name of a triple canoe; three canoes rigged abreast.

stranger, to let us first go and have a sea-bath, then, when we come back, we will feel refreshed, ready to compare our skill."

Moemoe replied: "You had better go and bathe yourself; the dirt is so thick on you that it is caked, as if you had always slept in the dirt, and just came down here to shake the dust, and spread it like a cloud of smoke rising high, and overshadowing our backs."

Iwahaonou was filled with anger, because he was told that he was so dirty, the dirt had caked on him.

He stood up and said: "You wait here for me, and when I return, we will have our sport, but if I return and you are gone, I will follow till I find you and I will crush you for bait to catch sharks with."

"I shall be delighted also to meet you and test our skill and strength, and you will see how I will bend you like the twigs on the tree; not one twig that a bird can rest on, green or dry, will be left, and that is how I will bend your bones," Moemoe answered.

After Iwahaonou had left, the assembly began discussing the affair of Moemoe and Iwahaonou.

Then Moemoe asked the people: "Are you well acquainted with this man?"

They said "Yes, we all know him. He lives up Napuu and he often comes to bathe in the sea."

Moemoe told them that this was not a human being; he had a shark body and a shark mouth is on his back, and that is why he wears that Pa'upa'u (g) cloak to hide his back.

That is the shark that is eating all these people who go down to the beach to bathe or fish.

(g) Pa'upa'u—Old, worn out kapa (cloth), filthy, dirty.

When he sees them going down, he then comes along and engages them in conversation.

"You are going to the sea-shore?"

"Yes, we are going for a sea-bath."

"Yes, the shark hasn't had his breakfast yet."

"That man with the shark body who has gone down, is not really going sea-bathing. He has gone to eat those people who have gone fishing for opihi, crabs and to dive for wana (sea eggs).

We will hear the sad news, today, that those people have all been eaten up by the shark. The country will be depopulated, if you do not kill this man-shark. If you do not believe me, prove it yourselves by catching this man; and take good care he does not get away, and also be careful how you grab him in the back, or his great shark mouth will bite off your hands."

Moemoe told them to build an unusually large imu, and when it was ready, and the man-shark had been cooked, they must be very careful how they throw out the pieces of unburnt wood, and see that the ashes or anything from the imu does not get wet with the salt water, for if it does, this man-shark will come to life again.

Let us learn a little more about Iwahaonou, the man-shark. He lived at a place called Puaka-hale at Puuana-hulu, the latter a hill not unlike Diamond Head in outline.

He lived there, and planted sweet potatoes, taro, sugar cane and bananas, and the road to the beach was alongside of his home.

As the people passed by, he would call out: "You are going to the beach?".

They would answer "yes."

"The shark hasn't had his breakfast yet! Do not take

any sugar-cane named Hui, for that sugar-cane is kapu, belonging to Hui, the Shark-God of this coast."

The people paid no attention, but continued on their way to the beach. When part way down below the pali (precipice) Kapaala, and lower down near the cave of Naalu, they would hear these words being called after them:

"They are carrying the Hui sugar-cane."

Then they would throw the cane away, and a great stack would be found along the road near this cave of Naalu.

Now this Iwahaonou talking to these people and explaining about the sugar-cane of Hui, was Hui himself, the Shark-God. When the people had gone on to the beach, he would rush down, and arrive there first, and pretend to be watching the Chiefs playing konane, and chuckle to himself over his cunning ruse. This had happened several times, and quite a number of people had been eaten by the shark; never suspecting this man was a man-eating shark; and terror reigned all over the land.

Let us return to the people who had followed Moemoe's instructions in preparing the huge imu, ready to cook Iwahaonou, and were waiting for him.

In the meantime, they heard screams and wailings of the men, women and children being devoured by the shark.

As soon as Iwahaonou appeared before Moemoe and the people who were waiting for him, at a nod from Moemoe, the men jumped and caught him, and as he was struggling, another lot came, and helped hold him down and tied his feet and hands; and when they took off his old dirty cloak; sure enough, there on his back was the huge mouth of the shark wide open, his sharp teeth showing, and his eyes ablaze like balls of fire rolling from side to side.

While he was lying there, Moemoe summoned all those men whose wives and children had just been eaten by this man-shark, to throw him into the imu. Almost immediately after he had been thrown into the red hot imu, he was cooked to a crust and crumbled into a heap of ashes.

That was the end of the man-shark and the people were safe to fish and bathe in the sea thereafter.

This land of Napuu was and is now a very large division of land, and was well populated in ages past, and it was largely cultivated for the Alii Keawe-Nui-a-Umi (Great King Keawe, son of Umi). Ehu was appointed Chief of this division, and for the reason of Ehu peacefully governing here, the saying has been celebrated in songs descriptive of Kona which has been handed down to the present day as "Kona I ka La'i a Ehu," (Kona in the Calm of Ehu); also "Kona Kaimalino a Ehu," (Kona of the Smooth Sea of Ehu).

THE POND OF WAINANA'LII

Wainana'lii (The Water Belonging to the Chiefs) was considered the largest and most celebrated fish-pond on the Island of Hawaii, in fact, the largest in the whole group; said to contain an area of 600 acres or more. It was situated near Kiholo. On a map published in the Paradise of the Pacific magazine, May, 1925, Wainanarii (a) is written on the Western coast of Owyhee, as the Island of Hawaii was then called. The map was published, according to the Paradise of the Pacific, London, November 7, 1843, by John Arrowsmith.

So it shows, this pond must have been of some note before the great flow of 1859 destroyed it. The great lava flow of 1859, not only filled and destroyed this pond, but formed a lava promontory extending out into the ocean.

A legend is told of two young girls who were stationed as guards over this great fish-pond.

They were kupua, wizards, and had two forms, a human and a lizard one. They were often seen in their lizard form sunning themselves on the stone wall of the pond.

One day these two girls were in their human form, and had just returned from a swim in the sea, and were drying their flowing tresses, when the Goddess Pele who had come down the slope of Mauna Loa, and had crossed over, and was racing down from Puuanahulu to destroy the Fish-Pond

---

(a) Wainanarii—The foreigners who first came to the Islands, always spelled words, using r for l; t for k, and b and d, which are not in the Hawaiian alphabet.

of Wainana'lii; she seems to have had a mania for destroying fish-ponds; spied these two beautiful girls, and before they could move, she covered them with her mantle of lava.

Kaniku (ku means standing) and Kanimoe (moe means lying down or sleeping) are now two lava slabs, side by side, and as their names indicate, one erect and the other flat, just as Pele had caught them.

These two lava slabs are on the old trail across the lava flow of 1859, and twenty-five and thirty years ago, this rough trail was the only road one travelled along the coast between Kona and South Kohala. The trail was marked with the bones of animals who had fallen on the way, and also with white coral stones.

In sections of this trail, on ancient lava flows, are markings, (Petroglyphs) representing ancient Hawaiian myths and history.

Pele seems to have respected these marks of history; they may have represented some eulogy in her favor; and so spared them. No one will ever know, though, how many she may have ruthlessly covered.

ILLUSTRATOR'S NOTES

Frontispiece: On the mountain, Pele, the volcano goddess, was young and beautiful, but on the shore she became ancient and angry. The face of this wrinkled and balding luahine (old woman) shows the bone structure of youth. Even today it is considered unwise to refuse food to an old woman on the coast.

Opposite Page One: Looking westward toward the sea at dawn, Akahipuu can be seen below and a suggestion of Kuili in the distance. The rooster is a jungle fowl common in those days.

Page Twelve: The well-rounded figure of this country girl typifies the Hawaiian concept of beauty. She is wearing a tapa pau (skirt) and her long hair shows that she is unmarried. Wawaloli has the physique and curly hair of the ideal warrior of olden times.

Page Eighteen: The plants in the foreground are dry land kalo (taro), growing at the edge of a banana patch. The adz wielded by the father is the kind said to be used for hollowing logs. The dog shown in the picture is the poi dog. It no longer exists and was drawn from descriptions.

Page Twenty-Four: Among the inshore warm water fish, the manini (surgeonfish) is easily recognized by its black bands. It feeds on seaweed about ten feet deep and may be netted but not hooked. Salted sundried manini is delicious with poi (the Hawaiian staff of life made from cooked taro corms.)

Page Thirty: Drought in Kona meant not only little drinking water but famine as well. Staple food plants, such as taro and sweet potatoes, died. Fish, pigs and birds either quit the area or were harder to catch. The houses of this type were used in this location at the time of Captain James Cook's visits.

Page Thirty-Four: The bald kahuna (priest) is making nae (fishing net) with the tools of his time, differing from those used for this purpose today. The tree above him is uulei, the slender branches of which furnished the best means of spreading fine net in the water. The spider used for scale is the harmless orb.

Page Thirty-Eight: The shark is mano niuhi, the man-eater, said to reach a length of thirty to forty feet. Some divers say the most fearful thing of all is having this shark above you. There is no escape. This is how it is pictured.

Page Forty-Six: This petroglyph field is an imaginary one, a composite of similar fields found in the desolate Maukele of Puna and the Kiholo area in Kona. The unending billows of smooth pahoehoe lava were inviting canvasses for travelers.

L. R. McBride